BLACK OBSERVATORY

BLACK OBSERVATORY

poems

CHRISTOPHER BREAN MURRAY

JAKE ADAM YORK PRIZE | SELECTED BY DANA LEVIN

MILKWEED EDITIONS

Published 2023 by Milkweed Editions
Printed in Canada
Cover design by Tijqua Daiker
Cover artwork by Otto Marseus Van Schreick
23 24 25 26 27 5 4 3 2 1
First Edition

Library of Congress Cataloging-in-Publication Data

Names: Murray, Christopher Brean, author.
Title: Black observatory : poems / Christopher Brean Murray.
Description: First edition. | Minneapolis, Minnesota : Milkweed Editions, 2023.
    | Summary: "Christopher Brean Murray turns his powerful lens toward the
    strange darkness of human existence in Black Observatory, selected by Dana
    Levin as winner of the Jake Adam York Prize"-- Provided by publisher.
Identifiers: LCCN 2022028466 (print) | LCCN 2022028467 (ebook) | ISBN
    9781639550265 (paperback) | ISBN 9781639550272 (ebook)
Subjects: LCGFT: Poetry.
Classification: LCC PS3613.U7584 B57 2023 (print) | LCC PS3613.U7584
    (ebook) | DDC 811/.6--dc23/eng/20220702
LC record available at https://lccn.loc.gov/2022028466
LC ebook record available at https://lccn.loc.gov/2022028467

Milkweed Editions is committed to ecological stewardship. We strive to align
our book production practices with this principle and to reduce the impact of our
operations in the environment. We are a member of the Green Press Initiative, a
nonprofit coalition of publishers, manufacturers, and authors working to protect
the world's endangered forests and conserve natural resources. *Black Observatory*
was printed on acid-free 100% postconsumer-waste paper by Friesens Corporation.

CONTENTS

ONE

TWO

THREE

FOUR

BLACK OBSERVATORY

ONE

A WELSH SCYTHE

is better than a Swiss lathe
or a Scotch spade. I wouldn't think
of using a Norwegian adz
or an Austrian sledge unless
it was clear that a Welsh scythe
was not available. Once I employed
a Belgian T square, which was enlightening,
though the results were less than impressive.
The Greek panel saw loaned to me
by a neighbor was hardly worth my time,
but in his garage I spotted a Slovenian radius trowel,
and that helped me in ways I could not have predicted.
Avoid Polish jackhammers and Finnish gimlets.
These items are not only dangerous,
they're addictive. And rude. The French chisel
is a charming device. If the Welsh scythe did not exist,
this tool would be worth considering.
But it does exist. Therefore, I advise you
to fling the French chisel into the Seine
next chance you get. Yesterday
a man was bludgeoned with a Serbian mallet.
But that is not so surprising.
A famous sonnet was once written
about the Portuguese linoleum knife.
Still, the poet was third-rate, and he hanged himself
with the garter of his former mistress.
Spanish forceps: I acknowledge their originality and verve.
They could easily seduce a naive journeyman.
I, however, remain unconvinced
by the Italian whipsaw, the Hungarian bench plane,
the Danish spike bit, and the Russian boilermaker's hammer.

In the 17th century, a brief skirmish
was fought over the Swedish putty knife.
But that is, at best, a footnote in a forgotten history book
glazed with dust in a blind machinist's basement.
Much more significant was the appearance
of the Bulgarian ploughshare. Few now recall
the scandal prompted by this apparatus,
but I assure you: in its day it was radical.
As for the English, what have they given us but the grease gun?
And so, I, an Irishman, straddle this lonely heath,
gripping my grub ax, dreaming of a scythe from Wales.

LETTER TO KNUT

Knut, what do you want me to do
with all of these boxes? Why did you keep
so many? Most of them are empty.
One's filled with photos of someone else's life.
Knut, whose life is it? I thought I saw you
in the shot of the mossy fountain.
There's a blur of dog leaping for a Frisbee.
There's a guy laughing who looks like
Robert Kennedy. You didn't know Bobby,
did you? You would have told me.
This box is full of soccer uniforms. Knut,
that's just weird. Or were you a coach?
Is that where you went when you disappeared
before dinner? Were you doing sprints
with the kids? You were thinner
with each passing day. Did you leave your pipe
on the bench? Had you finally put down
that volume of Spengler? It looks like
someone hacked this box with a machete.
Were you angry? Why didn't you tell me
when we were roommates? All those days
you spent shut up in your room, you could've
talked to me. I know I threw fits sometimes.
I didn't mean to shatter your viola. I offered
to buy you a new one. I know: *It cannot be replaced.*
Knut, are you okay? I want to know.
I'm alone in the house. It's starting to snow.

SPARTAN GAVOTTE

A constellation shivers in the firmament.

Clavichord notes ricochet from a dome inscribed by anguish.

Archetype of the jay—it's nonetheless drawn to seed.

A fire in the distance calls our names.

It calls through the tangled boscage.

Do you know the man in severest suit? Did you

invite him? Give him your phone number?

In the attic there's a painting that's both fictional and true.

It depicts a holy rebellion.

A blood-flecked arm extends a flare into darkness.

The darkness vaults on like a highway, like a fierce bird

whose wingspan embraces an impossible girth. One of its feathers

is released from earth. It interrogates the dusts

of an undiscovered planet. Still, farm life continues.

Sky bathes the wheat stalk on which the polished beetle dreams.

Cables, alive with information, crisscross in the soil.

A man, hunched over a page, strains to pronounce a word.

How can it help him? Can it stem the tide?

The tide fists onward, tenderizing the beach.

It washes a crab into a high shelf of weed. It rinses the hand

flayed by fishing line. Another tide courses through the cables.

Neither is more political. Neither cares a jot.

Far away a man is led to a field and forced to kneel.

He kneels a long time.

A logging truck plowed into the side
of his car, decapitating the young writer,
crushing his spleen, truncating his promising
career. His first book, a novella, had just appeared.
The critical response was enthusiastic.
He'd been called "an Appalachian Chekhov
with Roth-like resonances." That blurb and others
adorned the backside of his volume.
The authors who praised him were the masters
of the day. On the glass-strewn passenger seat
rested a blood-splattered manuscript,
a collection of stories titled "Summer at Strange Lake."
The margins were scribbled with notes
that would clarify to the editor the author's intentions.
All of this we knew from public radio.
But it was months before we realized
that we'd moved into the house he'd once occupied.
At first, I thought nothing of the sounds
from the cellar. I assumed that the old furnace
clicked as it struggled to warm the rooms.
Yet, when I ventured down the steps
in search of the fuse box, I was startled to see,
under a bare bulb, a Smith Corona on a makeshift
writing stand. A typed page said, "I listen to the footfalls
on the floor of the room above me. I eavesdrop
through the walls on their conversations.
Their lack of self-awareness is charming and tragic."
Was it an unfinished story? I sent the pages
to his publisher. Months passed. Katherine and I
went about our lives. We enjoyed leisurely dinners,
but we both worked hard in the daytime.

She rose at five. My work was part-time,
so I tended the garden and made repairs to the house.
One November day, I was on a ladder, removing leaves
from the gutter, when I glimpsed a man glaring at me
through the rain-spattered window of our room.
Regaining my balance, I looked—but he was gone.
I didn't tell Katherine. She was under pressure.
Reports were due, an evaluation was coming up.
Some nights, as we lay in bed, I listened to the gusts
that flung rain against our windows,
that havocked the wind chimes dangling
from the porch ceiling, that made leafy boughs
drum on the sides of the house. However,
now and then I would sift from the array
an errant thump that could not be attributed
to the wind. Once, as my consciousness surfaced
from the dream-confused depths of sleep,
I thought I heard the chime of a spoon
against a teacup. I sat up. Katherine didn't stir.
Had I left the kitchen light on? No cup
rested on the counter. I couldn't tell whether
the spoon had been used. A copy of *Hard Times*
was splayed on the table. Had Katherine been reading it?
She'd once ranted about how boring she found Dickens.
And she had no time to watch even her favorite show.
I never asked. She was irritable. Over time,
these events were eclipsed by her promotion, then
by the pregnancy. Having almost forgotten the dead writer,
I was startled one day to see a new, posthumous work
in the window of a bookstore. It was called
The Man at the Window. My pages were not included.

HALLUCINATED LANDSCAPES

1.

Someone finds a spear on a dune at dawn.
The beach town's streets are silent.

2.

Rain drums on my roof for an hour.
From the window I survey the bay.

3.

Two days drift like ammonia
under the nostrils of an unconscious waif.

4.

Gulls conspire in the blue
to descend upon a herring shoal.

5.

The wharf is popular with foreigners
and youths wielding scissors in their souls.

6.

I bike past cornflower blue houses
where old men on porches

7.

nap in vaults of shade. I pass a large horse
painted white on the globes of its eyes.

8.

When I stop at an intersection,
a cat tickles my ankle with its whiskers.

9.

A whiff of borscht on the breeze,
but let us hurry forward—the day is big with fate!

10.

A canoe, upturned, would provide solace
from the sun's persistent glare.

11.

An antiquated system is updated.
A heraldic crest adorns my beret.

12.

As I pedal, a woman smiles at me
from the mirror of a parked car.

13.

Machinery clangs. A miniskirt
is pinched between a streetcar's doors.

14.

In an attic, a man thumbs a yellowing
diploma, an anonymous love letter.

15.

A mackerel slices water,
barreling toward the meal it will become.

16.

At vespers, we arrive in a village
where a jukebox blares in a roadhouse.

17.

The spear is gone from the dune.
So are the footprints of the one who retrieved it.

18.

Summer arrives like a hot rivet
in hot sand under a vast moonless sky.

GET SEGOVIA

If you're going to hire a guitarist, get Segovia.
Not Andrés. The other, younger Segovia.
He's not related. He's hated by purists
for his irreverent solos. He wears bolo ties
and snakeskin boots. His fingers shoot
down the neck at lightning speed. He pursues
the essence of a Bach minuet with a sort of
artistic greed. Half of him doesn't give a fuck.
The other half needs to chase the sublime
like a hound pursuing a fox into a thicket
shattered by moonlight. Once I heard him
turn Schubert into a blues using a penlight
for a slide. A couple rose and left the theater
in a huff. Others expressed gruff criticisms
in the lobby. I enjoyed the piece, though
I had front row seats, and Segovia was gassy.
It was a small price to pay. Another time
he plucked a raucous César Franck. Somehow,
though he played an acoustic, feedback flowed
from the rear of the auditorium. When the piece
ended—his fingers tripping playfully down
a staircase of notes—I demanded more of him.
Not because he'd let me down, but because
I was drunk and couldn't face the blank page
of sobriety. He suffered from notoriety. At first
he enjoyed it, but then it affected his playing.
His fugues lacked staying power; his arpeggios
were uninspired. He was mired in the crowd's
expectations. He tried playing loudly, matching
the notes with his nicotine-frayed voice. That
was a bad choice, but at least he was searching.

Once, in the middle of a Brahms, I saw his hand
lurching uncontrollably up and down the neck.
He collapsed, his guitar in splinters. The audience
cheered. Flashbulbs strobed their oblivion.
Had he forgotten what age he was living in?
He got wise, lay low, and practiced. Soon
he was back on tour, playing smaller venues.
His menu was the same: Paganini, Grieg, and Schumann.
And still, he dressed like a bluesman. He's got the fire,
and I recommend him without reservation.

ENDLESS DICTATIONS

pour over the roof tiles of the house
on the outskirts of the city we lived in
before the war dispersed our possessions
to the winds that scour the horizon
or swirl within the abandoned swimming pool
where we floated as we were bronzed
by the sun that warmed the soil
inducing seeds to crack and sprout
and soon the whole region swelled
fruits were ushered to market upon the heads
of the local women who laughed
and some went with young soldiers
one of whom was killed by a girl's bitter brother
a knife in the gut was jerked upward
until innards spilled yet sublime music
filled courtyards even the old hermit
emerged to depict the festival in watercolors
that did not so much describe the sky
as dictate its possibilities to the day
which was long and heat-drenched
and filled with hope though events
would unfold regardless of desires
the young husband who today vaults
the laughing child to his shoulders
tomorrow drowns his skiff flipped
by a fist of wind his shattered bride
will either adapt or perish like the indigo
butterflies migrating to their usual spot
and finding it paved they flutter from one
fence to another until a decision is made
and they vanish like a fleeting thought

AN ENCOUNTER

I was lying in the hammock
when I heard a distant handclap.
I sat up. A tanager alighted on the bough
of a conifer. A fawn traced the perimeter of
my yard. My boots were mud-splattered.
I headed for the thicket, pausing
only to pull my machete from its sheath,
which was nailed to the wall of my garage.
I heard babbling, as if a baby
lay in the brush. A baby
lay in the brush. I cropped his bangs.
He was a good baby. He grabbed my nose
and spoke in the vernacular of babies
who have a lot to say without words.

I emerged from the woods
onto a cobblestone road. Each stone
had a word etched into it. One said, "Premonition."
Another, "Admiral." The sky
was blue. A plane buzzed by
pulling a banner with no message.

I was enjoying my journey
on that road, not knowing who'd made it.
Maybe it just appeared one afternoon
during the Civil War. Snow was dusting
the steaming corpses. Who chiseled words
into the stones? Who put grasses in the fields
and fish in the pond I fished

as a child? I dropped hunks of peach
off the raft. Fish rose and ate them.
Was it good for them? Maybe
it wasn't. In the clearing

a campfire crackled. A shaman
stood beside it. He danced a jerking jig
that spooked me. I tore off my shirt
and threw it on the fire. I chucked my boots
into the woods and flailed madly,
chopping sprigs from saplings, kicking clumps
into the brush, shouting obscenities
at the mute firmament that sprawled overhead
like an idiotic defendant at a murder trial. He was guilty
and I didn't give a fuck. There was nothing

to be done. I poured a bucket of blood
over my head. I punted a cantaloupe
and screamed soccer scores
at my dead father. A microbus
idled by the road. The shaman
was in the driver's seat. I climbed in,
shut the door, and waited for him
to speak. We sat in silence. Then
we sputtered down that road of words
toward who knows what.

TWO

CRIMES OF THE FUTURE

Parking an opinion in cyberspace without a permit.

Listening to an unorthodox symphony.

Raising your voice to the representative of a transnational corporation.

Planting seeds in unapproved soil.

Laughing at a masterpiece in public.

Ingesting "freelance berries" picked at a mountain pass.

Looking someone too intently in the eye.

Sketching a beardless Jesus.

Copulating under a cloudburst in a windstorm.

Mimicking the voice of a newscaster.

Quitting a job everyone agrees you should keep.

Conversing meanderingly for several hours on a weekday.

Commiserating with the enemy's losses.

Goose-stepping through a graveyard in autumn.

Stroking the hair of a good-looking child.

Insinuating the limitations of science.

Kissing a foreigner at a time of war.

Taking up a musical instrument after the age of thirty.

Talking to a dog as if it were a human.

Drinking water directly from a lake or stream.

Hoarding tracts of undeveloped land.

Spreading rumors about a theme park.

Forgetting to take your medication.

Remembering the failures of your nation.

Burning the biography of a decorated historian.

Making unverifiable predictions.

MERRIWEATHER

I first heard his name in passing. Someone
was rinsing coffee from a spoon, saying, "That's just
how Merriweather is. . ." I was new to the city.
I was emailing my CV around and smiling politely
at new faces. I noticed that people really deferred
to this Merriweather—his first name? A man I met
at a potluck had camped with Merriweather in Patagonia.
Merriweather had gotten him and his friends
out of a jam when the stove gas ran low and a sharp sleet
hemmed them in for days. Another guy explained
that Merriweather had secured for him and his fiancée
a cherry farm where they could have the wedding
they'd dreamt of. Merriweather's band played,
and his bass solos shook bits of hay from the dusty catwalk.
People danced and cried out to Merriweather for more,
then laughed as a bale tumbled from the loft,
just missing the sweat-drenched drummer. Couples
snuck off to the guest cabins, and a young woman
claimed the pomegranate punch tasted like starlight.
A boy found a silver dollar on the freshly laid macadam.
Merriweather's band debuted a Sam and Dave tune
they'd rearranged so that people looked at each other like
What the fuck, how can they be this good? During the break,
Merriweather spoke to a woman about her father's death.
She was moved by how closely he listened
and by the questions he asked that showed he understood.
She inquired whether Merriweather was married.
No one knew. Someone had glimpsed him
at the wharf with a much younger woman.

The two stared across the bay toward Bronson Island where wild boar still roam and clusters of purple lichen hang from the limbs of the spidery trees that vivisect the tarnished sunlight. Tears filled Merriweather's eyes and the unreal eyes of the young woman beside him.

THE WHITE SANDS MOTEL

1.

Here there's no rainy season.
Sun scalds my forehead,
yet the pool is empty. Beside it,
a toppled table, its glass surface shattered.
The asphalt is too hot for bare feet.

2.

Far away: white hillocks
and white dunes under a deep
blue sky. Swirling winds rake grooves
into the dunes. A glass of wine
in one hand, I lower my binoculars.

3.

An old man sweeps sand
from the motel's lobby. Still,
sand is everywhere: in my blazer's pockets,
under the glass of that photograph,
on my plate of tangerine sections.

4.

What do I see through binoculars?
The charred remnants of a campfire?
A vermilion lizard skittering
across a dune? A putrefaction on the sand
resembling a man? I sip my wine.

5.

The brochure says: ". . . a continental breakfast
served each morning." So I rise,
shower, shave, and tuck a handkerchief
into my breast pocket. In the lobby:
a dish of mints and a cup of coffee.

6.

The neon sign reads "No Vacancy"
in a violet looping cursive. So where
are all the guests? Today a boy in sunglasses
knocked on my door. He tried to sell me soap
from the housekeeper's cart.

7.

No carpet covers the floor of my room.
The mattress is excessively firm. No lamp.
At night, my room is dark. Sometimes,
however, the moon shines through
the sand-scratched glass of the skylight.

8.

Last night I dreamt that a man
was traversing a desert with a glass crutch.
A fox followed him, occasionally
trying to steal it. Angry, the man
struck the fox, shattering the crutch.

9.

I couldn't get back to sleep. A neighbor
kept me up. I heard something
like a jar of pennies being poured
again and again into a brass chalice.
I lay in bed, staring into the dark.

10.

The conference was canceled.
I could barely understand the message,
so poor is my phone's reception.
I punched the glass over the fire alarm.
I stitched my knuckle with black thread.

11.

How long have I been here?
Why was I sent without colleagues?
Is there a town nearby with a nightlife?
Where are all the women? How many pairs
of glasses could be made with all this sand?

12.

Today a new President will be inaugurated.
You would never know it by sitting
in the lobby. The lugubrious concierge
stares at the TV. But the TV is off.
Reflected in the glass: miles of white sand.

A HISTORY OF CLOUDS

You can think while walking, running,
washing the dishes, reading, grocery shopping,
or sleeping. Driving across Nevada at night
breeds thoughts. They leap from sagebrush
like jackrabbits into your high beams.
Most people can't think while writing.
They have ideas, yes, but not *thoughts*.
Anyone can snatch an old idea out of the dust
and show it around. Trying to think
will invariably prohibit thought. I thought
of writing this poem while driving to work
this morning. I made sure not to think about it
much. The wind swayed a stoplight
until it turned green. A man in a tank top
leaned into the window of a parked car.
It was not yet 8 a.m. Wisps of cloud
coursed through the sky over Houston.
Someone should compile a book
called *A History of Clouds*. It could be,
among other things, an anthology
of descriptions of clouds, from novels,
from the love letters of exiled princes.
Shakespeare's "pestilent congregation
of vapors" speech would appear, as would
Mayakovsky's "The Cloud in Trousers."
Clouds aren't mentioned much in the Bible.
God did, however, call to Moses from inside
a cloud. Enoch speaks of "the locked reservoirs
from which the winds are distributed."
Crane's "To the Cloud Juggler" and
Stevens "Sea Surface Full of Clouds"—

and that passage from Gogol
where a cloud slithers over Nevsky Prospect.
It stretches and coils and becomes an intestine
embracing the anxious protagonist
until we realize he's being suffocated by his thoughts.
Somewhere Rilke speaks of "vast, ruined
kingdoms of cloud." That from the love letter
of another exiled prince.

After the symposium, I walked toward my hatchback. I had a pebble in my loafer, so I stopped to remove it. As I leaned against a car, I noticed something in the back seat. It looked like a leg brace adorned with purple feathers. A leash coming off it led to a lump on the floor over which a silver apron was draped. I thought I heard a squeal muffled behind glass, but maybe it was an alarm in the distance. I stared into the car for a moment, then I moved on. I was supposed to meet Julie at the bowling alley for dinner, but now I thought I might drive out of town, find a motel to crash in for a while, watch an old John Cusack movie on cable, or else buy a novel at a drugstore, read the whole thing in one night, then go across the street for waffles. Today I read in *USA Today* that we secretly poisoned our own soldiers on purpose. Also, they're going to do laser surgery on the ozone layer or something. They had a picture of that actor accused of stabbing his son to death. In the photo (a still shot from his new movie), he brandishes a knife before the terrified face of a teenage girl. Later, as I walked past the shelter, I saw a girl who looked like the girl in the movie. Her hair was different, but her face was the same. I looked at her, and she looked back as if she recognized me. But I was late, so I hurried on. I lit a cigarette, then threw it away. I called Alphonzo and got his voicemail. He never picks up. I don't know why. As I was thinking that, he called to say he was going out of town. I asked if he'd received the package. He said no. I said it was on the way. He said okay. It started to rain. Then the sun came out. It was still raining when I drove to the symposium. Afterwards, I didn't query the speaker, nor did I head for the motel. I decided to go to the bowling alley to meet Julie. I would order the fish 'n' chips deluxe. I'd had it before. Then a squirrel leapt off the sidewalk into the street.

THE HAUNTED COPPICE

At the end of the dead-end lane
clogged with burr-shagged tangles
and pricker-studded stems, within earshot
of the trickling rivulet that probes the margins
of the warehouse district, one encounters
the inauguration of a path. At first,
it's just a strip of moss between rotting logs
infested with termites. Then a discernible track
of packed dirt snakes through fern-growth
under rioting constellations of gnats. Finally,
a clear trail appears and hugs the rim of a culvert.
It meanders indecisively through larch-shade
before diving underground and emerging
in a chirping thicket. I strolled that track
many times in my youth, slicing at skunk-leaves
with a switch, inventing—with my comrades—
frightening myths that peopled the coppice
with oracles and outcasts. One tale followed
the exploits of a deceased soldier who wandered
the forest in search of his misplaced sidearm.
When my friends and I found a petrified boot
amidst thistle, we recalled that somnambulant
grunt. A neighbor's spaniel would accompany us,
sniffing the trail, scurrying forward before pivoting
to make sure we followed. Didn't that trail
lead to the black observatory that hummed
like a power station beside a secret landing strip?
Didn't an estuary appear through foliage,
its cobalt waters cleaved by a white yacht's hull?
Colin, in his brogue, claimed the yacht transported
papyrus scrolls scribbled with esoteric maxims.

I said the crew passed a chalice infused
with the blood of a sacrificed saint. We argued
until dusk. Then we got lost. Only the shining
arc lamps saved us. At table, with my parents,
I sipped from my chalice, my hair smelling of ferns.

MY TIME WITH SPEECE

was odd. He was hired to install sod,
but he did it at night. Did he work
by moonlight or use a silent generator?
Once, he passed my window
as I rolled over. Our eyes met,
but I looked away. I heard the spray
of what sounded like twenty sprinklers
chittering in a stuttering dance. I was
entranced and felt he was competent.
Yet, when I rose, he was gone,
and the lawn was nonexistent. I found
a thin belt of sod draped over my mailbox.
I uncovered a cheap novel and a flashlight
behind my garage. Was he using me?
I had criticisms but suppressed them
as he pulled up at bedtime in his company's
gaudy van. "My man!" he exclaimed,
extending his fingers for a handshake.
I obliged, but he sensed my reservation.
He said he would take his lunch break early
if I didn't mind. I spied on him from inside.
He sat in the van, though he didn't seem
to be eating. He just stared ahead,
as if inspecting a crack in the windshield
or a distant blood-smeared horizon. But
there was no crack, and it was already dark.
He sat there for an hour. I showered
and read some psalms aloud. I wasn't proud
when I parted the blinds again.
The van was gone. No sign of Speece,
nor any indication that work had been done.

The pot of ferns by my door was missing.
He never returned, so I couldn't confront him.
Summer rolled on. Rain turned my yard
to mud. I couldn't help thinking of Speece—
why had he done this? I dreamt of him
several times. He'd stroll up to my door
with a bucket of blood he said he'd found
at the bottom of the lake. I looked up,
saw his mask, his eyes laughing
through the slits. The dreams stopped
when I sold the house to cut my losses.
I moved to a condo several towns away.
One day, I received a postcard scrawled
in purple ink, the handwriting of a child.
On the front was a waterfall in Oregon.
I tried to read the script, but it was a havoc
of marks, the spelling virtually indecipherable.
After wading through what seemed some
kind sentiments, I realized it was his bill.

FIELD

I came to a field
of grasses I couldn't name.

A puddle reflected
an overcast sky. By a stone wall

I glimpsed a wiry bush
with sharp, crimson flowers.

I sat down and inhaled, though
the air was polluted. All air

is polluted now. My head
was filled with chatter, memories

of people I'd hurt, hours spent
roaming a bookstore

only to depart empty-handed.
I was hoping to find the volume

that would reignite the flames
that engulfed the house

I grew up in, the barn
behind it, the acres of woods

I roamed with my dogs.
Let it burn, it's already

gone. Let flames take
the books I loved

and lived in for years
as I walked the streets of Missoula,

human conflagration
of desire and doubt,

anxiety's plaything
in a Soul Asylum T-shirt—

he didn't know he'd chosen
a path to a field of unraveling.

THREE

THE NEW AMERICAN PAINTERS

They stroll through town in pigment-
streaked shirtsleeves. They've allowed
their hair to grow long. Without exception
they wear beards. They laugh too loudly
at their own quips, at the too-precious
works of their predecessors. Though
they once conspired in private to overturn
the dominant paradigm, they now declare
their intentions in cafés. Often
they flee these establishments without paying
for their bowls of broth, their endless
espressos that cause the sky to pulse
with possibilities, which they hurry
to depict in oils slathered over monumental
canvases crammed into draughty studios
across whose bare wooden floors
empty wine bottles roll. Oblivious breezes
flip the pages of their sketchbooks.
One artist employs a makeshift easel
as another flings paint with eyes closed.
Some scoop dust from the floor
and smear it through clots. If that fails,
a canvas is cast to the ground,
its author stepping on it, spitting insults,
only to resurrect it and continue
the feverish brushstrokes, the breathless dance
toward then away from the canvas. Is it abstract?
It resembles the bald head of a screaming Incan
glimpsed from above. He wades through

drifts of peonies into which cobalt sky-shards
tumble. It's titled *The Codex*. I'm reviewing it
for *Artforum*, and the painters refuse to comment.
They just gesture toward it, as if its meaning is obvious.

THE INVISIBLE FOREST

I would've sworn it was a thriving
metropolis, yet pine-scented winds

rushed between buildings. I saw
a fawn lapping a puddle of rainwater

outside my apartment, but I was late,
so I hurried on, my moist hand

gripping the handle of my briefcase.
I stopped for a paper; the kiosk

was gone. In its place: a copper statue
of a commuter. He gripped a case

like mine. He wore a similar wristwatch.
Yet, in his other hand, he held a compass.

"Who's commemorated by this work,
and what has he to do with our city?"

I wondered, feeling I was being watched.
I ducked into The Uptown for my usual

black coffee. Constance smiled
as she handed me my change.

I located last night's scores. Only
in the street did I notice the mud

caked to my shoes. I stomped it off
and headed for the subway. A man

uttered something incomprehensible.
Another tried to sell me a receiver

yanked from an ancient phone.
I sipped from my cup. Its contents

startled me—like runoff from a glacier.
I tossed it and ran to make my train.

Billboards pictured athletic bodies
splashing themselves with a beverage.

A monitor showed a burning car
weaving through a crowd. I

pushed through the turnstile,
descended to the platform,

and poured with the others
into the over-crowded train car.

As the doors slid shut, I heard the coyote cry.

WITHOUT WINSTON

Without Winston, nothing is the same.
There's a sorrow I feel when I say his name.
Where'd he go? Is he hiking a glacier
toward a glistening shard of moon?
Will he return soon with a crate of limes
and gifts for all of the children? Perhaps
he's building shelters in a war-torn nation. Or maybe
the devastation he glimpsed caused him to retreat
to a monastery. Of course, he might have gone the other way—
say, to Vegas. Is he running numbers and consorting
with showgirls? Has he grown his hair out
so that blond curls spill across his shoulders
as he twists the arm of a man who hasn't paid him?
He seemed content in the days leading up to
his disappearance. He'd produced some stunning woodcuts
depicting the spidery trees of the orchard.
Yet, I thought I heard him crying
as I passed his office. When I knocked,
it stopped, and the light went off. I spoke his name.
No reply. I put my eye to the keyhole.
A breeze bathed my eyeball. I didn't see him inside.
Last time he left us, he wrote twice a month,
enclosing sketches and poems. This time all we've received
is an empty, unsealed envelope addressed in his manic cursive.
Were the contents removed, or was that Winston's message?

W. S. MERWIN

He talked for half an hour before reading a poem.

Time is illusory, he said.

It passes, but it also stands still.

He said there might be people on distant planets just like us.

That could be frightening, he said.

Or it could be wonderful.

He said his astronomer friend said the universe is much
    bigger than we can imagine.

He said the deconstructionists were wrong.

He said poetry is alive in South America.

People don't care if they don't understand it.

He said North Carolina is beautiful—tell no one.

He said people read more poetry now than when he first
    started writing.

He said listening comes first, then seeing.

He read a poem about a blind man who held seashells
    in his hand.

He read a poem about a frog who was a believer in rain.

He read poems inhabited by the ghosts of trees.

Waves of innocence usurped a boat.

Nameless voices undulated like the sea.

A silent cricket was the pupil of night.

He said humans are not special.

Animals have language, he said.

And we have imagination.

ABANDONED SETTLEMENT

We came upon it at midday. We needed
a rest. Our packs were heavy, and the trail
wove serpentine through mountain crags.
It looped through fields of stone
before tracing the lips of cliffs that hung
over the gaping abyss. Eagles coursed
the cloudless expanse. A lizard stared at us
before vanishing. Vegetation was sparse:
only stubble and scrub. Yet, at the settlement
we found shaggy spruces. We offered
a polite greeting to our anticipated hosts.
No answer. I kicked open a cabin's door.
It smelled of urine. On the floor: a soccer ball
and some thumbtacks. Above a bunk,
a picture of a woman spreading her sex.
She wore purple boots and a white derby.
Mouse shit speckled the floor. Otherwise,
the cabin was empty. We walked a trail
that hugged a creek into which someone
had hurled a mini fridge. Did we hear music?
We arrived at a firepit encircled by benches.
This, I guessed, was where the settlers met
to discuss the state of the tribe. Who were they?
On a bench I found a coin. One side pictured
an orb to which birds or angels flocked.
Below it stood a naked man, seen from behind,
his arms welcoming the tides that washed his ankles.
The other side depicted a battle, but the forces
resembled apes more than men. On the left,
one bit another's brow. Above the scene,
a scroll billowed. The phrase etched there

was in a language I didn't know. I put the coin
in my pocket and looked up: my companions
were gone. Their packs leaned against trees.
I called their names. Removing my pack,
I smiled at their prank and stepped toward
the backside of a cabin. I leapt to startle them,
but they weren't there. I found the door locked
and felt the first pang of fear. Their packs
were gone. I wrestled mine to my back
and followed a trail into a fern-strewn bowl.
The air was cool. A fawn regarded me
with apprehension. I found a trailer home
tucked into a shady nook. Between a tree
and the trailer was a dewy web on which sat
an ugly brown spider larger than my thumb.
I was careful not to disturb it. I knocked.
No answer. I entered, and from a radio
a woman said that her daughter couldn't sleep
after a road-rage incident. The host told her
to read a book his listeners would know.
I surveyed the room: an overstuffed chair,
a shelf clogged with books. The hallway
extended further than I'd thought possible.
My pack scraped walls. Past the water closet
was a curtain. I imagined that on the other side
a large, tattoo-streaked man performed oral sex
on his teenage daughter. He wouldn't be happy
to see me. Instead: a table and four monitors.
One showed foot traffic in a large city.
On the second, the spider weaving the web.
The third played a terrorist training video.
Men in black hoods scanned rooms
with guns. The fourth played a loop

of a car shattering a rail and hurtling
through a lot before plunging
off a cliff. *Why a loop?* I wondered. Then,
through the windows of the careening sedan,
I glimpsed the horrified faces of my friends.

THE WAYWARD BROTHER

Beware the wayward brother
with his fang of gold, his
cutoff T-shirt, his paperback copy
of *The Starr Report*. Beware
his ways, for once he's locked
onto you, you're an MiG fixed
in his feckless crosshairs. Where
did you meet him? Did he crash
your tailgate party, help himself
to a brat before butting into
the conversation? Which tale
did he recount? The one about
his stint as a roadie, the nubile
groupies he deflowered, the lyrics
he penned for the band? Did he
scan your face to glean your
reaction, clap your back with
a mustard-streaked hand? How
did your friendship extend beyond
that day? Did you see him near
your house, changing a tire?
Did he take you up on your offer
to help? Did you point to your place
just blocks away? When did he
arrive without notice? He had to do
his laundry someplace—where else
could he charge his phone?
When did it become *his* home?
When did he acquire your Harley?
Was he imparting wisdom to your kids
when he aimed a gun at the dog?

What happened to the cash in the pantry?
Do you need proof? Do you know
his past? Is that guy with the mullet
his friend? Did he lend your drill
to someone, or sell it? Who'll tell him
he can't smoke in the house? Was he
staring down your wife's blouse
as she spooned peas onto his plate?
What did he mean by, "I love me
some chicken"? Was he winking? What
was he thinking when he parked on the sod?
Does he believe you're made of money?
Or care? Will he draw the line? Beware.

DUKE & PAM

One thing I've never been able
to get into a poem is the way
I felt about my dogs I was
a kid & woke first on Saturday
came downstairs & slid
the glass door open to speak
their names into the blue
the barn uphill to the left
the pines silent all around
a hint of oncoming snow
within minutes Duke & Pam
would trot from the woods
my bare hands & feet chilled
I'd say *c'mon* they'd enter &
climb onto the torn couch
rear to rear & I would get
on top of them wedge
my feet between cold fur
& squeaking leather lie down
my cheek to fur & talk to them
listen to their grunting pleasure
as they licked & licked my hands

HOMECOMING

At the edge of town, you pass a water tower beside train tracks.

A shopping cart blocks your path.

The telephone poles have no wires.

Someone has spray-painted "Fuk Yo" on the train station.

A breeze bathes your face

as seedpods click overhead.

How long's it been since you sat in a theater?

The marquee says JAWS, but the ticket booth's empty.

The jewelry store says: 40% off weeding rings.

Brass clips clink against the flagless pole.

The library is a house that's rumored to be haunted.

The librarian recounts tales of the first settlers' deaths.

She's seen books flung from shelves,

a woman at the bottom of a staircase.

You pass a garage where mechanics yammer.

At the nursery, a sprinkler douses the curb, leaving shrubs parched.

A Corvette peels out in a mini-mart parking lot.

Smoke drifts over storefronts.

At the Dairy Queen, a woman buys cones for kids.

She snaps at them, but they remain buoyant.

At the football field, boys run plays.

The potbellied coach shouts, "Let's see some hustle!"

Cheerleaders practice a coquettish dance.

A middle-aged man watches them—the principal?

Past the ShopRite, the drugstore, the family restaurant,

the graveyard's as quiet as moss on stone.

Weather has worn away some names and dates.

Vandals have defaced a magnate's bust.

As a child, you wondered about what's underground.

Decaying uniforms from the Revolutionary War.

A soil-streaked skeleton, ring still on its finger.

One plot is new, the sod is fresh.

FOUR

ONCE, LONG AGO, IN A POEM

Once, long ago, in a poem, I wrote, "The lindens
are glazed with frost at five in the morning,
and we nod to the violet distance, its steeple
announcing the hamlet where the precocious youth
inscribed the map that induced his exile."
Once, long ago, I wrote that, and yet
there were no lindens. I lived near the desert
and worked for the government. I'd rented a room
above a dry cleaner. Mostly what I remember
is sitting in the one chair I owned, staring
at the stucco wall, listening to the Sri Lankan
dry cleaner argue with his wife, their ravaged voices
rising from a vent into my room. I imagined them
on the day before they left their homeland,
the thrilling hopes that might have kept them awake at night
on the humid subcontinent. Now they spend their days
inhaling that dry cleaning smell, drinking diet soda,
arguing with customers about stained blazers,
a TV yammering in the corner. Yet I knew little about them.
I wondered if I should go downstairs and introduce myself.
But I just sat there. Cars drove by. The machines
hummed. I tried reading for a while, but the novel
had lost its appeal. The characters had become
"characters." The novel had become "a novel."
I wanted the characters to be that couple downstairs.
I wanted a secret stairway behind my wall to spiral
deep into the earth. I wanted to be with the characters
so we could return together to the subcontinent to swim all day
in the lagoon so blue. That's when I wrote the poem.

SALVAGED TRAVELOGUE

We were in a wood of telescoping voices

There were no reasons in the grass

Under bark something whispered backwards it rained

The sky tipped the mountain the slope reddened clouds

The dog tensed & barked at déjà vu

Wires entangled your boot you yanked someone screamed

Before that the thermos went missing

We found the plaque that said he was here

The brick pump house whined & had no door

The trail led to the swimming pool in the woods

It continued on toward the black observatory

The rain was over there we were getting wet

The dog barked an hour slid a thermos can't just vanish

The ranger in the distance appeared to be praying

We heard voices no one was there

The dog ran into the woods & was gone a long time

Puddles reflected blue it was overcast

Something shifted in leaves not the dog

Had someone thrown something we found the thermos

We sipped coffee hotter than before

At a lookout one cloud flexed into the valley

We heard geese but couldn't see them

The thermos you asked again it was gone

The dog scraped your calf with the stick

The cloud appeared to glide along with us

The dog limped its paw bleeding

We saw winds shifting on the river

Now the pump house was silent

Someone had locked the gate

We heard voices the dog barked

Wires entangled your boot

BLACK OBSERVATORY

A man disappeared around the side of the observatory. I followed, but he was gone. I found only a propane tank and a rusted gardening tool. Through the fence and hedgerow, I glimpsed a copper-colored sedan parked across the street. Its engine started, and it sped away. The sky was cloudless. I imagined planets beyond the moon's clipped fingernail. Where was the astronomer? Swimming in the observatory's underground pool? There was a red planet with a violet ring painted on the pool's black floor. The water was heated by solar panels. Birds crapped on them. The birds built a nest in the telescope, but the astronomer set out poison. He wasn't in the pool when I arrived. A white ball bobbed on its surface like a moon. Was he sending messages with lasers to the inhabitants of other planets? Was he scanning the heavens with the telescope, hoping a comet would shoot through his retina into the star-smeared void of his mind? Perhaps he was asleep upstairs though strolling through the space station in his dream. I emerged—exhausted and thirsty—from the pool. I slipped a few silver moons into the soda machine in the hallway. It dispensed a can with two bottoms.

MEYER LOST AN EYE

but that didn't faze him. His outlook
was grim but inspiring. His diatribes were
tiring yet true. He was bold, unpredictable,
and hilarious. His multifarious talents
were deeply strange. Once, on the firing range,
he told me he'd assassinated a cloud. I laughed
and cast him a sardonic glance. But reflected
in his only eye was a bulbous white zeppelin
crashing behind the hills in the distance.
Was I in a trance? Meyer just smiled
and slid his rifle into its case. He left
as if nothing miraculous had transpired.
He wasn't mired in the world's mundane
machinations. He asked me to help him
with his Petrarch translations. I told him
I wasn't qualified. Yet he coaxed my opinion
about every turn of phrase. I was amazed
when I realized that I'd helped him enormously.
He'd drawn out of me something I didn't know
existed. I predicted that there would be
a warm but violent windstorm that evening,
and there was one. Shutters banged, and the dog
fled to the basement. An enormous tree limb
crashed through a casement. Though this magic
was fun, it was terrifying. Meyer just glared at me,
his empty socket cupped by a patch. His good eye
was like the fierce sweeping beam of a lighthouse
atop a jagged spit of land. It was less a helping hand
than an indignant reproach, especially as he began
to drink. Snifters were strewn about the house.
I heard him splitting open the pinewood cases

full of burgundy. Where would this lead?
Wasn't his work suffering? When I asked him,
he laughed and gestured—like he was winking
the lid behind the patch. I didn't know
how to take that. I left him to his own devices.
I studied the prices of silver, wheat, and coffee.
I tried to influence them. But Meyer made a racket.
He laughed into curtains and talked to the spines
of books. In the crook of his arm, he balanced
a curtain rod. On his head he wore a place mat.
He performed heartbreaking monologues with the hearth
as his backdrop. I couldn't stop him, so enthralled
was I. Most were impromptu, but one was familiar.
I crouched on an ottoman and listened, staving off
an encroaching fog of dread. He played every part
in the drama, including a king and a blind prophet.
His characterizations were brilliant. The emotion
was deeply felt. One speech rose to an unbearable
climax. Then with the rod he put out his eye.

FROM A LETTER

Something I heard today reminded me
of that passage in one of Flaubert's letters—
the silver lichen he glimpsed in the woods as a boy.

Later, after parting some vines, he emerged
onto a lawn behind a cottage, the home perhaps
of a merchant busy haggling with townspeople

over prices, or enumerating for them
the curative properties of a powder
to be mixed with milk. On the lawn,

young Gustav saw a woman, the wife
of that merchant. She lay on a chaise longue
dragged into the grass. He stood still

and watched her resting in the sunlight,
her dress pulled up above her knees,
her chestnut hair splayed over a pillow.

He watched her in the silence, fearing
she would notice him, or was he anxious,
knowing the moment would pass?

Her bare white arms had blond hair on them
and a light kidney-shaped birthmark.
A wren alighted on a post nearby.

The lilac's scent had dissolved
on a breeze that shimmered the leaves
of a faraway tree, and as he thought this

her eyes opened, returning his gaze.
Then they closed, and she continued resting.
He waited a moment before returning home.

REMNANT SHOWROOM

As we entered, we noticed on the desk
a paper plate on which lay a half-eaten slice
of meatloaf, an ear of boiled corn, a scattering
of lima beans, and a few cornbread crumbs.
The chair was empty, the attendant nowhere in sight.
Yet I was certain I'd scheduled our visit for today.
Over the phone, I thought I'd heard a party.
The man who'd taken our reservation
was interrupted by a woman with a high voice.
He would cover the receiver mid-sentence,
then they would laugh as the mouthpiece
scraped his coat buttons. That coat, which had three
brass buttons, lay on the floor. On a card table rested
two half-filled plastic champagne glasses
and an ashtray in which lay a saliva-moistened
cigar stub. On the desk was a clipboard,
and on its single sheet was scrawled
a name similar to mine, but longer
and more Slavic-sounding. Beside the name:
the word "Too." I looked at my watch.
It was 2:04. My colleagues and I waited,
examining our phones, craning our necks
to peer down a dark hallway. Eventually,
the attendant emerged in gray trousers
and an undershirt. His suspenders swung
around his thighs. "You're early!" he bellowed.
He grabbed the clipboard and asked me
to sign. As I did, he slipped on his rumpled
blazer and ran his fingers through his hair.
From somewhere came the female giggle
I'd heard on the phone. I handed him

the clipboard. He bowed and gestured
toward some saloon doors. Unlike the lobby,
the showroom would not have been out of place
in a first-rate museum. The floors
gleamed. Light shined not from bulbs
but from flat, chemical panels that reduced the glare.
A uniformed guard sat in the corner.
His raised chin gave him a dignified appearance,
yet his holster was empty. The longer
I stared at him, the more I wondered
whether he was made of wax. He blinked.
I almost bumped into a pedestal. On it rested
several slates into which fossils were etched.
The textures of leaves had been pressed
into the stone, patterns of circulatory
and respiratory systems underscored
by the hooking swipe of a stem,
like a cocky flourish in a founding father's signature.
Also pressed into a slab was a dragonfly.
Had it landed on a leaf unaware
that it would be rendered immortal
by geological events? It had probably dreamed
only of nectar, like Keats. On my right,
under glass, was a cylinder of black plastic
tapering toward the middle and connecting
to an ornate segment of silver and jade.
Above it hung a photo of FDR laughing
at his or another's witticism. From his teeth
jutted the cylinder into which a cigarette
had been inserted and lit. Was his DNA
still on the plastic marked by his teeth?
To my left, a weathered footlocker's
faded labels announced where it had been:

Moravia; Bhutan; Portland; Brussels; Cincinnati;
Dakar. Its lid was open. Inside, the possessions
of the traveler: a suede sack with a purple silk
tie-string, a long brass blade with an emerald handle,
various blouses with ruffled collars and cuffs,
Spanish leather boots that were too small
for any man responsible for hauling this trunk
onto the deck of a galleon setting sail
for bustling lands at the edges of the known world.
I noticed a daguerreotype that depicted
the diminutive sailor in the very vestments
contained in the trunk. He glared into the lens,
his sun-blistered face gleaming, his eyes
exhibiting an exemplary resolve. Beside him
stood a woman twice his size and half his age,
her breasts brimming over her bodice, her gaze
cast upon him with admiration and desire.
The corner of the image had been singed,
perhaps in the conflagration that took the lives
of these lovers? The placard explained
only that the man had discovered
the island of Buaggi, near Western Samoa.
The guard was staring at me, eating an apple.
I moved to the next exhibit: a page
torn from the journal of an explorer.
The ink was smeared, as if he'd been
a lefty. From the ornate script I deduced
that the pioneer had arrived in an uncharted zone
whose terrain resembled the surface
of a distant planet. The soils are described
as "Reddish, yet not red." The cliffs: "Stone-like,
yet pliant." The rubble was somehow edible
to the "birdlike creatures that arrived in waves."

The author describes some berries the creatures
disregarded but which, when muddled,
produced a violet solution like India ink.
A colleague coughed. He straddled a stuffed horse,
mimicking the Pony Express officer
painted on the adjacent wall. I inspected
a red lacquered box on which were stenciled
urban scenes: raucous festivals, fierce battles,
an execution, a coronation. The placard noted
that this was the coffin of King Kebbatau IX.
I was sure the placard should have said
the chest had been *removed* from Kebbatau's tomb.
Yet, inside it was the child-monarch's skeleton.
The ribs were twigs. Surmounting the skull:
a crown studded with rubies. Both femurs,
which lay on a black velvet bed, were fractured.
A gold band encircled a finger. A gold tooth
featured an inlaid diamond crescent.
Had he worshiped the moon, or did he convert
to Islam? A colleague touched my elbow.
I nodded, and we moved toward the exit,
past the splintered guitar of the famous musician
and Jackie Kennedy's blood-stained skirt.
Departing, I heard faintly that high-pitched giggle.

POEM FOR X

After scouring forests and fields,
After scanning the hollows of trees,
The back seats of burned-out sedans
Abandoned to the streets of New Jersey,
After ranting into a snaking gutter
Until echoes from the depths mocked
My useless complaints, after reviewing
My choices and revising my defense,
After compulsory apologies to myself and others,
After evicting the squatters and confronting
My oppressor, who was myself, after letting go
The thing I had, the lovely thing that shined,
The thing that danced with a spontaneous verve
Coursing from the root of life,
The thing that foundered and was broken
But which I gripped desperately in the rain
At oblivion's cusp, rivulets loading my pockets with silt,
Which might have fostered growth
Had I not cast handfuls to the wind
And spat anguish into ditches. After all of this,
I stepped forward and found you. The past has collapsed
Like a fortress of earth. I don't know the future.

JAUNT TO VERMILION

Went there. Was frisked. Found
in the dirt the leg bone of an elder.
Sent it home. Rinsed my feet
with wine. Imbibed a glass of sky
on a wrought-iron balcony in the rain.
Recited a psalm outtake. Shook a maraca
filled with teeth. Bit a lime. Arrived on time
for the execution of a bad idea.
Faked a slow blues at a weathered piano
on the back of a truck racing south
toward Jackson. Cashed my chips in.
Ducked the taxman. Axed the flaxen
trunk of a birch which I stacked
before the fire that warmed my hands
chilled by the Arctic winds ushered in by
El Niño. Ate a lamb. Ran toward the Tropic
of Cancer. Planted a chip in my hand
to monitor my blood before the next
election. Sought protection. Was rejected.
Was nevertheless protected by the fact
that nothing matters in the whole scheme
of Nature with its West Winds
and its clattering ash-boughs soon crusted
with ice. Was stabbed twice. Laughed then
at the corrupt ceiling in a Demerol dream
and followed an elk to a shale-strewn
precipice. Was dictated to by
an untraceable voice. Made a choice.
Chose a jaunt to the red horizon.

ACKNOWLEDGMENTS

Poems in this collection have appeared in the following journals:

American Poetry Review: "Crimes of the Future," "Remnant
　　Showroom," and "The White Sands Motel"
Bateau: "An Encounter" and "Salvaged Travelogue"
Bennington Review: "Field"
Cimarron Review: "Duke & Pam"
Colorado Review: "From a Letter"
Conduit: "Once, Long Ago, in a Poem"
Denver Quarterly: "My Time with Speece"
Fou: "Get Segovia"
Grist: "Poem for X"
Handsome: "Hallucinated Landscapes"
Hoboeye: "Black Observatory," "The Invisible Forest," and
　　"Letter to Knut"
The Journal: "The Squirrel That I Killed"
jubilat: "Jaunt to Vermilion"
New Madrid: "The Haunted Coppice"
New Ohio Review: "Abandoned Settlement," "A History of
　　Clouds," "Homecoming," and "Merriweather"
North American Review: "The New American Painters" and
　　"The Wayward Brother"
Pleiades: "The Ghost Writer"
Puerto del Sol: "Meyer Lost an Eye"
Rattle: "W. S. Merwin"
Salamander: "Endless Dictations"
Third Coast: "A Welsh Scythe"
Washington Square Review: "Spartan Gavotte"

Thank you to my teachers, fellow writers, & friends from the University of Houston's Creative Writing Program. Thank you to Kevin Prufer, whose help with this book was indispensable. Thank you to the late Tony Hoagland. Thank you to Mark Levine. Thank you to Rich Levy, Krupa Parikh, & Inprint Houston. Thank you to Tam Armstrong, Ben & Nancy & Victoria Tiffany, Susan Thomas, Deniz & Dean Tuck, Geoffrey Nutter, Hans Koch, Nadya Pittendrigh, Kerri Hecox, & Gillian Engberg. Thank you to Bettina Murray & Renee Tobin. Thank you to the journal editors who published poems from this book. Thank you to the late Mitch McInnis. Thank you to Wayne Miller & Dana Levin. Thank you to everyone at Milkweed Editions. Special thanks to Joe Fletcher & Earl Craig.

CHRISTOPHER BREAN MURRAY has received awards from the Academy of American Poets and Inprint Houston and he served as online poetry editor of *Gulf Coast*. His poems have appeared in *American Poetry Review, Colorado Review, Copper Nickel, New Ohio Review, Washington Square Review*, and other journals. He lives in Houston, Texas.

The Jake Adam York Prize for a first or second collection of poems was established in 2016 to honor the name and legacy of Jake Adam York (1972–2012). York was the founder of *Copper Nickel*, a nationally distributed literary journal at the University of Colorado Denver. His work as a poet and scholar explored memory and social history, and particularly the Civil Rights Movement.

The judge for the 2022 Jake Adam York Prize was Dana Levin.

milkweed
EDITIONS

Founded as a nonprofit organization in 1980, Milkweed Editions is an independent publisher. Our mission is to identify, nurture, and publish transformative literature, and build an engaged community around it.

Milkweed Editions is based in Bdé Óta Othúŋwe (Minneapolis) within Mní Sota Makhóčhe, the traditional homeland of the Dakhóta people. Residing here since time immemorial, Dakhóta people still call Mní Sota Makhóčhe home, with four federally recognized Dakhóta nations and many more Dakhóta people residing in what is now the state of Minnesota. Due to continued legacies of colonization, genocide, and forced removal, generations of Dakhóta people remain disenfranchised from their traditional homeland. Presently, Mní Sota Makhóčhe has become a refuge and home for many Indigenous nations and peoples, including seven federally recognized Ojibwe nations. We humbly encourage our readers to reflect upon the historical legacies held in the lands they occupy.

milkweed.org

Milkweed Editions, an independent nonprofit publisher, gratefully acknowledges sustaining support from our Board of Directors; the Alan B. Slifka Foundation and its president, Riva Ariella Ritvo-Slifka; the Amazon Literary Partnership; the Ballard Spahr Foundation; *Copper Nickel*; the McKnight Foundation; the National Endowment for the Arts; the National Poetry Series; and other generous contributions from foundations, corporations, and individuals. Also, this activity is made possible by the voters of Minnesota through a Minnesota State Arts Board Operating Support grant, thanks to a legislative appropriation from the arts and cultural heritage fund. For a full listing of Milkweed Editions supporters, please visit milkweed.org.

Interior design by Tijqua Daiker and Mary Austin Speaker
Typeset in Jenson

Adobe Jenson was designed by Robert Slimbach for Adobe
and released in 1996. Slimbach based Jenson's roman styles
on a text face cut by fifteenth-century type designer Nicolas Jenson,
and its italics are based on type created by Ludovico Vicentino
degli Arrighi, a late fifteenth-century papal scribe
and type designer.